MOMENTS OF DEVOTIONAL AND PRAYER

Laurie Joyner

AuthorHouse™
1663 Liberty Drive
Bloomington, IN 47403
www.authorhouse.com
Phone: 833-262-8899

New International Version (NIV)
Holy Bible, New International Version®, NIV® Copyright ©1973, 1978, 1984, 2011 by Biblica, Inc.® Used by permission. All rights reserved worldwide.

New Living Translation (NLT)
Holy Bible, New Living Translation, copyright © 1996, 2004, 2015 by Tyndale House Foundation. Used by permission of Tyndale House Publishers, Inc., Carol Stream, Illinois 60188. All rights reserved.

ISBN: 978-1-6655-2566-4 (sc)
978-1-6655-2567-1 (e)

Print information available on the last page.

Published by AuthorHouse 05/19/2021

authorHOUSE®

Dedication

In memory of my mom Cheryl Joyner-VanStory who has suddenly passed away on February 9, 2021. The pain I feel knowing that I cannot spend another moment with or talk to my mom, has been awfully hard. My mom was my biggest cheerleader. She supported me in everything I did. I could always count on her honest opinion, inspiration, encouragement, and dedication to all my endeavors. We talked about everything together. I did not keep anything from her and of course because she was my mother. I am still highly adjusting to her not being here with us any longer. This is a road that I never thought I would ever have to experience; I honestly was not ready for her to go to glory but who is ever ready? I miss and Love my Mama very much!

GOD has not forgotten about you. Regardless of any chaos or any distractions, anything that may be going on around you, know and believe the LORD has a plan and purpose for your future. Keep believing, keep praying, keep trusting the LORD, and keep walking by faith.

Sometimes when we think that our understanding is right, we can find ourselves in anxiety because things are not happening the way that we want them to happen and, in all actuality, things will only happen for us according to the master's plan that he has for our lives.

Journaling

_____

_____

_____

_____

_____

_____

_____

_____

_____

_____

_____

_____

_____

_____

_____

Psalm 139:14, NIV:

I praise you because I am fearfully and wonderfully made;
your works are wonderful; I know that full well.

Ephesians 2:10, NIV:

For we are God's handiwork, created in Christ Jesus to do good
works, which God prepared in advance for us to do.

Luke 12:7, NIV:

Indeed, the very hairs of your head are all numbered. Don't
be afraid; you are worth more than many sparrows.

You are fearfully and wonderfully made. Masterpieces never decrease in value. You are HIS workmanship created in CHRIST JESUS. All the hairs on your head are numbered and you are more valuable than sparrows. Be sure you are adhering to the standard of priceless GOD called you to be!

Journaling

_____
_____
_____
_____
_____
_____
_____
_____
_____
_____
_____
_____
_____
_____
_____

Isaiah 46:4, NIV:

Even to your old age and gray hairs I am he, I am he who will sustain you.
I have made you and I will carry you; I will sustain you and I will rescue you.

You are POWERFUL! Be strong in the GOD. Remember that it is his might that will carry you until old age, not your own.

Put on the full amor of GOD that is provided in CHRIST JESUS. Stand strong as you lean on GOD and what JESUS has done for you, not in your own strength.

Journaling

_____
_____
_____
_____
_____
_____
_____
_____
_____
_____
_____
_____
_____
_____
_____
_____
_____

Today I would like to take this opportunity to stop everything that I am doing to praise the creator. Won't you praise him along with me?

Thankful to you GOD for who you are. Thank you for your grace, agape love, mercies, and unmeasurable favor! You are so awesome, so powerful, and such a gracious God! I Love and adore you LORD, will never place no one or thing above you. You are my King, my ever-lasting GOD, the Great I am, and I am stronger with you in my life every day! Thank you for your Holy Spirit, thank you for your wisdom, thank you for restoration, thank you for your peace, and thank you for your awesome Truth! Bless your Holy name Father GOD, I give you all the praise, glory and honor, amen!

John 17:20-23, NIV:

"My prayer is not for them alone. I pray also for those who will believe in me through their message, that all of them may be one, Father, just as you are in me and I am in you. May they also be in us so that the world may believe that you have sent me. I have given them the glory that you gave me, that they may be one as we are one in them and you in me so that they may be brought to complete unity. Then the world will know that you sent me and have loved them even as you have loved me.

GOD will show himself strong when we pray, trust, and believe. Having faith in him activates his promises. JESUS is our source to get our prayers to the father, we are one, we also have the glory, were brought in complete unity with the father through JESUS. As we pray let us be reminded of the love GOD shares for us as well as the love that he has for JESUS, which will show himself strong in a mighty way. We are one.

Journaling

_____

_____

_____

_____

_____

_____

_____

_____

_____

_____

_____

_____

_____

_____

_____

Joshua 6:20, NIV:

*When the trumpets sounded, the army shouted, and at the sound
of the trumpet, when the men gave a loud shout, the wall collapsed;
so everyone charged straight in, and they took the city.*

Acts 16:26, NIV:

*Suddenly there was such a violent earthquake that the foundations of the prison were
shaken. At once all the prison doors flew open, and everyone's chains came loose.*

Psalm 34:18, NIV:

*The LORD IS CLOSE TO THE BROKENHEARTED
and saves those who are crushed in spirit.*

No matter what comes up against you this week worship GOD, things happen, things change. I decree and declare when you worship GOD, walls are torn down. I decree and declare chains will break. Hearts are mended and spirits are renewed.

Journaling

_____
_____
_____
_____
_____
_____
_____
_____
_____
_____
_____
_____
_____
_____
_____

Matthew 11:28, NIV:

"Come to me, all you who are weary and burdened, and I will give you rest.

In today's world allowing the peace of GOD rule your heart is so especially important. It may seem as a hard task as we are faced with a lot of uncertainty and stress; but as we choose to trust GOD rather what we may be encountering we will find ourselves in peace as we rest in him. This is an act of will for us amen. Victory is yours if you choose to trust GOD today.

Journaling

_____
_____
_____
_____
_____
_____
_____
_____
_____
_____
_____
_____
_____
_____
_____

Encouragement

I decree and declare this week will be a great week for you!

I declare the favor of GOD in your homes, to change your life, and your families lives, Breaking generational curses and full of wisdom and great health.

I decree and declare that you will be prosperous, joyous, full of JESUS' agape love which will transfer to overflow on all you encounter.

I decree and declare A big life, we serve a big GOD, with wonderful new opportunities you were not even expecting!

I declare GOD'S divine favor of alignments in your circle to flourish as you evolve into the plan that he has for your life. New opportunities to be established by the work of your hands this day and every day on forward. I Speak the full favor of GOD to surround you all the days of your life. In JESUS name amen.

Romans 15:4, NIV:

"For everything that was written in the past was written to teach us, so that through the endurance taught in the Scriptures and the encouragement they provide we might have hope." ... And the Scriptures give us hope and encouragement as we wait patiently for God's promises to be fulfilled."

Due to the pandemic, we are not allowed in the church house due to safety precautions. As we know we are the church it is also necessary to be revived to hear from a preacher as well. The Bible should be preached it is a divine commission that is sent by the lord to preach the gospel, it is necessary. Online services are available because of our current situation with this worldly pandemic. Get your blessing. Praying and searching the scripture has its solutions and gives you hope. Hope to your questions, and hope to your concerns.

Journaling

_____
_____
_____
_____
_____
_____
_____
_____
_____
_____
_____
_____
_____
_____
_____

Ephesians 6:10, NIV:

Finally, be strong in the Lord and in his mighty power. Put on the full armor of God, so that you can take your stand against the devil's schemes. For our struggle is not against flesh and blood, but against the rulers, against the authorities, against the powers of this dark world and against the spiritual forces of evil in the heavenly realms. Therefore, put on the full armor of God, so that when the day of evil comes, you may be able to stand your ground, and after you have done everything, to stand. Stand firm then, with the belt of truth buckled around your waist, with the breastplate of righteousness in place, and with your feet fitted with the readiness that comes from the gospel of peace. In addition to all this, take up the shield of faith, with which you can extinguish all the flaming arrows of the evil one. Take the helmet of salvation and the sword of the Spirit, which is the word of God.

Life's challenges and changes can drain you of your drive and certainly your power but let me encourage you today to stay connected to the real plug. Our source that keeps us energized and full of hope to dream, amen! Get recharged by connecting to JESUS, The real plug for power. Reconnect today and be strong not in yourself but in the LORD.

Journaling

_____

_____

_____

_____

_____

_____

_____

_____

_____

_____

_____

_____

_____

_____

_____

_____

2 Samuel. 22:33, NIV:

*It is God who arms me with strength
and keeps my way secure.*

Today take courage in the LORD! Whatever is front and center in your mind be encouraged. It will not win this battle if you invite JESUS into it. Do not let doubt or fear trick you into stress and anxiety. I decree and declare by inviting the LORD in this battle your strength will be increased and your way will be made perfect, so be of good cheer.

Journaling

_____
_____
_____
_____
_____
_____
_____
_____
_____
_____
_____
_____
_____
_____
_____
_____

Encouragement

He is my El Shaddai.

He is my Jehovah Nissi.

He is my Jehovah Tsidkenu.

My Jehovah Shammah

So, I do not ever have to worry about him being anywhere else, I am never alone because he promised to be present in every situation with me.

He is omnipresent.

He is my Jehovah Rohi

He's my Jehovah Shalom and I live in Great Peace.

Hebrews 11:6, NIV:

And without faith it is impossible to please God because anyone who comes to him must believe that he exists and that he rewards those who earnestly seek him.

My prayer is that JESUS be with you in such a special way as you seek him, you cannot help to notice his presence, that you cannot help but to feel and see his love displayed as you follow wherever he leads you. "Whoever would draw near to God must believe that he exists and that he rewards those who seek him". God himself is our greatest reward. And when we have him, we have everything. Therefore, "Seek the Lord and his strength; seek his presence continually!" Daily tell him JESUS, I trust you for every part of my life. You will begin to see him in every situation of your life.

Journaling

_____
_____
_____
_____
_____
_____
_____
_____
_____
_____
_____
_____
_____
_____
_____
_____

Psalm 138:8, NIV:

The L<small>ORD</small> <small>WILL VINDICATE ME</small>;
your love, L<small>ORD</small>, <small>ENDURES FOREVER</small>
do not abandon the works of your hands.

GOD will move in the mist of your storm. I hear the LORD saying stay close to me I am freeing you from the chains that have held you back. I shall fulfill the promises that I have made to you. His love endures forever.

Receive it.

Journaling

_____
_____
_____
_____
_____
_____
_____
_____
_____
_____
_____
_____
_____
_____
_____
_____

Isaiah 55:8-9, NIV:

"For my thoughts are not your thoughts,
neither are your ways my ways,"
declares the LORD.
"As the heavens are higher than the earth,
so are my ways higher than your ways.
and my thoughts than your thoughts.

Let him turn to the LORD, and he will have mercy on him, and to our GOD, for he will freely pardon. "For my thoughts are not your thoughts, neither are your ways my ways, declares the LORD. "As the heavens are higher than the earth so are my ways and thoughts that your thoughts.

Journaling

_____

_____

_____

_____

_____

_____

_____

_____

_____

_____

_____

_____

_____

_____

_____

_____

Jeremiah 33:3, NIV:

*Call to me and I will answer you and tell you great and
unsearchable things you do not know.*

I decree and declare that GOD is going to visit you and your family with supernatural answers that you have been looking for. I hear the LORD saying call out to him!

Journaling

_____
_____
_____
_____
_____
_____
_____
_____
_____
_____
_____
_____
_____
_____

Psalm 33:4, NLT:

For the word of the LORD IS RIGHT AND TRUE;
he is faithful in all he does.

God is the author of our lives. He is our portion, and all the strength we need. Our identity can be found in the LORD as we spend time with him. He will plant our hearts with truth. I decree that the word of GOD will transform your life and all fear will be cast away. GOD is faithful.

Journaling

_____
_____
_____
_____
_____
_____
_____
_____
_____
_____
_____
_____
_____
_____
_____
_____

Luke 1:37, NIV:
For the word of God will never fail.

As we know because of his great track record GOD will always come through to give us strength when we think that we cannot go on. When we are discouraged, he will give us joy? When things looked impossible, with him it was made easy. We serve a good and all-knowing GOD.

Journaling

_____

_____

_____

_____

_____

_____

_____

_____

_____

_____

_____

_____

_____

_____

Nehemiah 8:10, NIV:

Nehemiah said, "Go and enjoy choice food and sweet drinks, and send some to those who have nothing prepared. This day is holy to our Lord. Do not grieve, for the joy of the LORD is your strength."

Praising God on today for his faithfulness. Every morning we decided to make the decision not to let anyone spoil our mood and put our peace first when we were tried. We were set on being more positive and ignored the negative. We let the joy of the LORD be our strength and we made it! Celebrate, you deserve it!

Journaling

_____

_____

_____

_____

_____

_____

_____

_____

_____

_____

_____

_____

_____

_____

_____

Phil. 2:9-11, NIV:

*Therefore, God exalted him to the highest place
and gave him the name that is above every name,
that at the name of Jesus every knee should bow,
in heaven and on earth and under the earth,
and every tongue acknowledge that Jesus Christ is Lord,
to the glory of God the Father.*

As you go through this week if you keep your eyes focused on the solid rock of JESUS, our anchor he would never budge or move on you, never sink, or give away to defeat. Our blessed assurance, he gives us mercy. He is our safety, gracious, forgiving, faithful, powerful, and strong tower.

Maintain a real relationship with JESUS and cultivate it. JESUS can see what is ahead so do not let go of his hand but believe in him and the greater works. Pray to JESUS he is LORD to the glory of the father.

Journaling

_____
_____
_____
_____
_____
_____
_____
_____
_____
_____
_____
_____
_____
_____
_____
_____

Prayer

I plead the precious Blood over our lives, over our families lives, our friends, our brothers and Sisters in Christ, and coworkers' lives. Father GOD, Break down these barriers that try to separate us from You and Your will for our lives. Protect us from every weapon formed against us, whether invoked or controlled by witches, warlocks, or Anything that is unlike you. The enemy is busy LORD keep him at bay Father GOD. Keep him out of our lives, away from our children, our family members, our jobs, our churches. Protect our minds from the manipulator, false imaginations, accusations, assassinations, or anything that disrupts our peace or causes discord. Help us to dream or pursue what you have already shown us LORD. Bless us LORD as we bear the cross. Thank you, JESUS, for peace, grace and mercy. This is my prayer I send in the matchless name of JESUS, amen!

1 John 1:9, NIV:

*If we confess our sins, he is faithful and just and will forgive
us our sins and purify us from all unrighteousness.*

If you going to be anything, be honest to GOD "First." The bible says, but if we confess our sins, he is faithful and just to forgive us our sins and to cleanse us from All unrighteousness.

Journaling

_____
_____
_____
_____
_____
_____
_____
_____
_____
_____
_____
_____
_____
_____

Isaiah 41:10, NIV:

So do not fear, for I am with you;
do not be dismayed, for I am your God.
I will strengthen you and help you;
I will uphold you with my righteous right hand.

Thankful unto God for allowing us to see this beautiful day.

Today, I want to remind you that you are blessed, you are loved by GOD. He cares for us and is always there for us, through any fear or dismay that we may be experience. He will strengthen us, help us, and uphold us (Isaiah 41:10 NIV)! The LORD has loved us with an everlasting love.

Journaling

_____

_____

_____

_____

_____

_____

_____

_____

_____

_____

_____

_____

_____

_____

_____

Encouragement

Our GOD is in the restoration business, and the Bible says that if we but confess our sins that he is faithful and just to forgive us of our sins and cleanse us of all unrighteousness. God will create in us a new heart and renew a right spirit within us, and I Decree and Declare that our Father is restoring you! I Decree and Declare that in this process of cleansing, of breaking down, he is chipping away, he is molding, he is shaping, and he is growing you! You were fearfully and wonderfully made! Sometimes we go down into the wilderness to the land of Egypt, and we get beat up and come out of there with the residue from the experience of being there. GOD had mercy and extended his grace, because he could have killed a lot of us when we were out in the wilderness, but instead he extended his mercy. In extended his hand of grace brushed us off for the cleanup, time to create in you what "He" needs of you for his plan that he has in store. To use of his glory!

It does not matter what people think all that matters is what God thinks! If you are pleasing him, you be happy with you, you should also be good to you! Always keep in mind that JESUS loves you! He is always there for us and wants the best for us. You best believe you can always count on him to protect us from the snare of the fowler. We can always lean on him! Believe in him, he is our strong tower, our rock and our sustainer, and there's NOBODY LIKE OUR GOD! He is our strength that we can always run to in a time of trouble. You just must believe in him and his word which never comes back void. Our GOD is a promise keeper, and he will keep you, just as he has always done for you in the past. He will do it again! Trust Him, Pray to Him, He's waiting on you and I am Praying for you too! I pray that your sleep be sweet tonight. GOD Bless!

Jeremiah 32:17, NIV:

"Ah, Sovereign L<small>ORD</small>, you have made the heavens and the earth by your great power and outstretched arm. Nothing is too hard for you.

I decree and declare.
New opportunities
New possibilities
New strategies, and
New favor in your life!
Our GOD has created all things, the heaven, and the earth nothing at all is impossible for our GOD. Get ready for your blessing.

Journaling

_____
_____
_____
_____
_____
_____
_____
_____
_____
_____
_____
_____
_____
_____
_____

Psalm 19:7, NIV:

*The law of the L*ord *is* perfect,
refreshing the soul.
*The statutes of the L*ord *are* trustworthy,
making wise the simple.

Today I am praying we decide to find answers to questions in the word of GOD. The word helps us to gain wisdom to make the best decisions according to GOD's will. The infallible word of God will assure us of all truth and to make conviction for change for better, transforming our mind for wise and simple choices. JESUS testimony is in the word which teaches and trains us When in doubt read the word.

Journaling

_____
_____
_____
_____
_____
_____
_____
_____
_____
_____
_____
_____
_____
_____
_____

Isaiah 49:16, NIV:

See, I have engraved you on the palms of my hands;
your walls are ever before me.

I hear the LORD saying, that he is with us. We should not worry, nor even fret this week. Our GOD is full of grace possibilities, love, and favor. We are his, we belong to him. He has us in the palm of his hands. GOD is about to do something unusual, something bigger than you ever imagined! Are you praying?

Journaling

_____
_____
_____
_____
_____
_____
_____
_____
_____
_____
_____
_____
_____
_____
_____

James 4:17, NIV:

If anyone, then, knows the good they ought to do and doesn't do it, it is sin for them.

As we go about our way on this journey, let us walk according to the will of the father. Sin of omission, not wanting to comply to GOD" S command or even his original plan and purpose is dangerous. GOD reigns! We must strive to be sure and give him everything within us that is good and release all that is of sinfulness. Let us strive in being pleasing to him daily, by helping build the Kingdom and not bring it down.

Journaling

_____
_____
_____
_____
_____
_____
_____
_____
_____
_____
_____
_____
_____
_____
_____

Psalm 24:1, NIV:

The earth is the LORD'S, AND EVERYTHING IN IT,
the world, and all who live in it;

GOD will teach us how we must rule over our circumstances. He is the ruler of us, the ruler of heaven and earth, the teacher of wisdom from challenges through the power of the word of GOD which helps us overcome. We are lifted in his presence, hidden from attacks of the enemy. The earth is the LORD'S. Declare his Lordship over all situations.

Journaling

_____

_____

_____

_____

_____

_____

_____

_____

_____

_____

_____

_____

_____

_____

Psalm 144:15, NIV:

Blessed is the people of whom this is true;
blessed is the people whose God is the LORD

My prayer for this week is that we make JESUS smile, in which will make us happy because he is our LORD.

Journaling

James 1:22, NIV:

Do not merely listen to the word, and so deceive yourselves. Do what it says.

John 17:17, NIV:

*Sanctify them by
the truth: your word is truth*

I decree and declare putting GOD'S word to practice will not be deceiving we will be doers of the word. Implementing great change in our lives, talking the talk, and walking the walk, surrendering in being sanctified to the word of GOD for demonstration of GOD'S truth because his word is truth.

Journaling

John 14:27, NIV:

Peace I leave with you; my peace I give you. I do not give to you as the world gives. Do not let your hearts be troubled and do not be afraid.

So grateful that we can rest in the peace that comes from JESUS. The peace that cast out all fear, the peace that triumphs any discouragement or anxiety, the peace that gives rest right in the middle of chaos.

Jehovah Shalom,
Thank you for being with us, and we can rest in you. Peace!

Journaling

_____

_____

_____

_____

_____

_____

_____

_____

_____

_____

_____

_____

_____

_____

_____

Psalm 139:14, NIV:

I praise you because I am fearfully and wonderfully made;
your works are wonderful,
I know that full well.

All of GOD'S works are divinely perfected. We are a miracle made. His proof of wisdom is shown to us daily. The LORD'S work of perfection is on display through us which is so incomprehensible. I praise him!

Journaling

_____
_____
_____
_____
_____
_____
_____
_____
_____
_____
_____
_____
_____
_____
_____

Psalm 23:4, NIV:

*Even though I walk
through the darkest valley,*[a]
*I will fear no evil,
for you are with me;
your rod and your staff,
they comfort me.*

Grateful that JESUS walks with us through all circumstances and difficulties. There is no evil to fear since we have thy rod and staff to comfort us. Angels are sent to protect us against the powers and principalities of this dark world, and spiritual forces of evil. Praise be unto GOD for being with us!

Journaling

_____
_____
_____
_____
_____
_____
_____
_____
_____
_____
_____
_____
_____
_____
_____

Prayer

Today I awoke with praise on my lips an attitude of gratitude.

Father GOD, I thank you! Thank you for being our El Elyon (The most High GOD), our Jehovah Raah (The LORD my shepherd), our Adonai (LORD, Master) our Jehovah Shalom (The LORD is peace), our Jehovah Nissi (The LORD my banner), and our Jehovah Rapha (The LORD that heals), our Jehovah Tsidkenu (The LORD our righteousness), our Jehovah Jireh (The LORD will provide), and our El Olam (The everlasting GOD), there is no other like you!

Thank you, for your strength and for your agape Love. Thank you, LORD, for your son JESUS you birthed through human flesh. Immanuel, GOD with us. Through JESUS we witness your life that flows through us. Redeemed by Immanuel who is divine and human in one.

I have a heart full of gratitude for the miracle birth of your son entering this sin infested ugly world that we live in here on earth, he claims us all as his own.

Thank you, for the blood of JESUS that brings us salvation. What a wonderful gift to be privileged to obtain.

I rejoice in the wonderful knowledge that Immanuel has come to rescue us, Amen! (Matthew 1:23)

Psalm 16:11, NIV:

You make known to me the path of life;
you will fill me with joy in your presence,
with eternal pleasures at your right hand.

Grateful that by being in the presence of the father we have pleasure and fullness of joy. The path of love from JESUS is such an honor to be able to enjoy. There is such warmth and brilliance in this path of display. The richness in growing to our understanding of it. Your way, your truth, and your light. Our eternal pleasures forevermore We are blessed!

Journaling

_____

_____

_____

_____

_____

_____

_____

_____

_____

_____

_____

_____

_____

_____

John 5:1-5, NIV:

Sometime later, Jesus went up to Jerusalem for one of the Jewish festivals.
² Now there is in Jerusalem near the Sheep Gate a pool, which in Aramaic
is called Bethesda[a] and which is surrounded by five covered colonnades. ³
Here a great number of disabled people used to lie—the blind, the lame, the
paralyzed. [4] [b] ⁵ One who was there had been an invalid for thirty-eight years.

The desire to change must come within the individual person by their own choice. You are wanting better for a person in particular area is great but them, their selves must have that same thirst. If they are not thirsty or not making any moves for greater, there is nothing you can do. Pray for them and accept it. They must want it for their selves.

Journaling

Matthew 6:33, NIV:

But seek first his kingdom and his righteousness, and
all these things will be given to you as well.

Seeking the father for all things that pertains to our lives is the breath of fresh air that it needs. Vitality, poise, love, just to name an important few. Marvelous deeds conspired on behalf of the father just for us because he cares and loves us. Seek the kingdom and his righteousness to come fall into fruition. When the father attends to our needs we can be ready, set in position for him to do exceedingly and abundantly more than we can ask or imagine. Seek him.

Journaling

_____

_____

_____

_____

_____

_____

_____

_____

_____

_____

_____

_____

_____

_____

Proverbs 18:17, NIV:

In a lawsuit the first to speak seems right,
until someone comes forward and cross-examines.

Luke 8:17, NIV:

For there is nothing hidden that will not be disclosed, and nothing
concealed that will not be known or brought out into the open.

The one who states his case first seems right, until the other comes and examines him. There are always two sides to a story. Investigate speaking to all parties before you make the determination. For nothing is hidden that will be made manifest, nor is anything secret that will not be known and come to light. Jesus never tried to work alone.

Journaling

_____

_____

_____

_____

_____

_____

_____

_____

_____

_____

_____

_____

_____

_____

Psalm 139.7, NIV:

Where can I go from your Spirit?
Where can I flee from your presence?

Thankful GOD will help us live in the light of all his truth. The LORD lives amongst us upon this earth we are destined for blessing beyond a hidden place. Nothing escapes his awareness so humbly we can come before him for freedom of sin, to be restored to his grace. I bind all fear running from the presence of his goodness and release trust and boldness, for deliverance, In JESUS name amen.

Journaling

_____

_____

_____

_____

_____

_____

_____

_____

_____

_____

_____

_____

_____

_____

_____

Matt. 19:20, NIV:

"All these I have kept," the young man said. "What do I still lack?"

John 15:5, NIV:

"I am the vine; you are the branches. If you remain in me and I in you,
you will bear much fruit; apart from me you can do nothing.

My prayer for this week is that we get to know the father better. More of a personal relationship with him. Spending more time with Christ JESUS our risen savior, a relationship void of just religion from childhood to adulthood, but of true authenticity. A relationship that will be full of growth and greatness in our lives only he can bring. It comes by hearing and reading his word and through prayer. We will become more intertwined with him, for he is the vine as we are the branches. Apart from him we can do nothing.

Journaling

_____
_____
_____
_____
_____
_____
_____
_____
_____
_____
_____
_____
_____
_____
_____

Phil. 1:6, NIV:

*being confident of this, that he who began a good work in you
will carry it on to completion until the day of Christ Jesus.*

Being thankful unto JESUS today because we can have confidence of this very thing that he will never abandon us. We can always depend on him to deliver, rescue, guide, show truth, and teach us. The Holy spirit grows within us to direct us into our purpose, our divine destiny of calling. GOD'S goodness serves great purpose for repentance. JESUS is our restorer, our healer, and our redeemer. I decree and declare that he which that begun a good work in you will perform it until the day of JESUS CHIRST in JESUS name, amen!

Journaling

Psalm 42:1, NIV:

*As the deer pants for streams of water,
so my soul pants for you, my God.*

Hebrews 4:16, NIV:

*Let us then approach God's throne of grace with confidence, so that we
may receive mercy and find grace to help us in our time of need.*

In this world of darkness cling close to the LORD. He will give you strength, to quench your thirst. Allow JESUS nearness to refresh you, to revive your soul from everyday life, the negativity and confusion that belongs to this world. GOD is not the author of confusion. The LORD will quench your soul just as the deer longs for water to revive him. I decree and declare the outpouring of GOD'S grace over you as you get closer to the throne in your time of need. In JESUS name, amen!

Journaling

_____
_____
_____
_____
_____
_____
_____
_____
_____
_____
_____
_____
_____
_____

Romans 5:8, NIV:

*But God demonstrates his own love for us in this: While
we were still sinners, Christ died for us.*

Just a reminder that GOD'S demonstration of love was shown through the sacrificial death of his son JESUS. In our sins the LORD saw beyond our human blindness and he made a way of escape for us. Grateful for his agape love, although wee deserved to pay the price. We should not take lightly he sent JESUS to spear us and for that let us be thankful in our days ahead, honoring, trembling in fear and reverence.

Journaling

_____

_____

_____

_____

_____

_____

_____

_____

_____

_____

_____

_____

_____

_____

Psalm 16:10, NIV:

*because you will not abandon me to the realm of the dead,
nor will you let your faithful[a] one see decay.*

Thanks be unto JESUS for not abandoning us to death, for not allowing us to die in our sinful nature but being an anchor. Giving us the promise of eternal life through the resurrection of CHRIST. Destroying all works the enemy has "tried" against us to bring death or lose hope and truth. Though there is sorrow in this life we have everlasting joy in heaven. Strengthen us to soar in the spirit, to endure life's trials and be sustained for the continuing of life's long journey. Eternal life of peace is in your presence, Amen!

Journaling

_____
_____
_____
_____
_____
_____
_____
_____
_____
_____
_____
_____
_____
_____
_____

Prayer

I Decree and Declare on today that GOD is going to supply all your needs according to his riches and glory by CHRIST JESUS. He will make a way, our GOD is able to do exceedingly abundantly above all that we ask or think, according to the power that worketh in us. He will make all paths straight, as he walks with us and talks to us. I pray that we are sensitive to the whisper of the Holy Ghost with in us which will direct our path. I Decree and Declare healing, deliverance, love, stability, peace, joy that surpasses all understanding, and an overflow of glory, comfort, and favor to go through rough places In the Name of JESUS. I speak new discoveries from our father in heaven, things that were unknown that our father will make known to us. Seeds of greatness, Glory to GOD! To be in contentment, be worry free, pursue who we were meant to be, a change agent, innovator, and a leader in boldness. I Decree and Declare that we will grow up in the ability to serve just like JESUS, to everyone we come across, every minute every hour, everyday Hallelujah!!! Heaven shall be on Earth! I rebuke the spirit of self-centered thinking and self-imposed limitations in the name of JESUS! Let us be perfected in the truth because the truth is what sets us free! I decree and declare that the love of CHRIST will work

through us to live in his way as true Christians on this Earth! Not to just say that we are Christians but let our actions taken place of what our mouths speak! I decree and declare that we will be true not just in the church house but outside the church house as well, and it is in JESUS'S name I pray Amen.

Psalm 63:1, NIV:

You, God, are my God, earnestly I seek you I thirst for you,
my whole being longs for you,
in a dry and parched land where there is no water.

Father GOD we are so happy that we have you in our lives. Every morning that we rise it is such a joy and honor to commune with you. We look forward to your great fellowship. We are rejuvenated upon entrance of your miraculous presence. Earnestly every morning we seek you our soul thirst for you because without you, cracks in our humanity begin to appear. Father GOD, where there is no water the soul longs for you in a dry and thirsty land. The heart yearns to love you more each day. You flood us with your refreshing waters from your fountain of living water. Thank you for a drink of your miracle waters of life.

Journaling

_____

_____

_____

_____

_____

_____

_____

_____

_____

_____

_____

_____

_____

_____

_____

Psalm 1:6, NIV:

For the Lord WATCHES OVER THE WAY OF THE RIGHTEOUS, but
the way of the wicked leads to destruction.

The LORD keeps his eye on us guiding our every footstep. Thankful that our paths have been designed by GOD. He has our plans mapped out. By faith, we follow as he is leading and guiding us to destiny. Mesmerized as his glory unfolds which he has prepared in our lives. Father GOD my prayers are for those that have rejected you. They need you LORD to shine your light on them so they might not perish, amen (Psalm 1:6 NIV)!

Journaling

_____

_____

_____

_____

_____

_____

_____

_____

_____

_____

_____

_____

_____

_____

_____

Deuteronomy 6:4, NIV:

Hear, O Israel: The LORD our God, the LORD is one.

"Yahweh Elohim" Our unique and powerful God! It is such a declaratory statement, there is none like you, no equal. Our one and only GOD from the beginning to the end. Our Majesty, Master creator, Godhead that holds all divine revelation.

Everything in this world that we see, all that we be, all that is formed, in all unity though one GOD which whom we worship.

He has called us into his presence and calls us his own. Oh, what a great privilege to be his child!

Our provision, our protection, our sustainer. Teaching us the wisdom of his ways and gives us hope that we can stand on. Let our love be a radiation to all we approach from the love GOD shines within us. We bless your Holy name LORD!

One GOD, one people. GOD bless us all.

Journaling

_____
_____
_____
_____
_____
_____
_____
_____
_____
_____
_____
_____
_____
_____
_____
_____

Romans 8:28, NIV:

And we know that in all things God works for the good of those who love him, who[a] have been called according to his purpose.

GOD'S wisdom is so huge, so great, way beyond our human comprehension. Adonai can turn any problem or situation we would ever face into a blessing. There is an opportunity to see through the lens of our father and learn in the obstacles that we face. As we approach them head on, prayer is essential to JESUS, being lifted above the circumstances for clarity of the lesson involved to be mastered for growth.

GOD is intentional for his glory, his purposes, making us stronger, wiser, and bringing us closer to him. Changing our heart, showing us the blessing in the mist of the struggle, so that we could grow through it, amen!

El Shaddai Is our healer, deliver, provider and our problem solver hallelujah!!! Always revealing his faithfulness in our situations. Opportunity is granted in each situation to apply the word of GOD and speak to mountains, allowing his promises to be revealed and crooked ways made straight, every valley be raised up, every mountain and hill made low; the rough ground become level, the rugged places a plain, amen.

GOD will always out smart anything that the enemy does, (Here comes the important part are you listening?) as long as we put it all in his hands. He makes it all for our good.

Journaling

_____
_____
_____
_____
_____
_____
_____
_____
_____
_____
_____
_____
_____
_____

Titus 3:5, NIV:

he saved us, not because of righteous things we had done, but because of his mercy. He saved us through the washing of rebirth and renewal by the Holy Spirit,

Being Thankful unto GOD this morning for loving us, not convincing or anything we have done, but by mercy, by grace. Thankful to be amongst the Kingdom as citizens, sonship, chosen, an ambassador for CHRIST JESUS, Amen.

Thankful for the Love bestow unto us that drew us to the cross of JESUS for salvation, accepting his forgiveness for sins, accepting him to be LORD of our life, for regeneration, we have been reconciled to GOD Glory to his name!

There isn't a thing, nothing at all that we could do for him to Love us anymore than he does. We are sinners being washed clean becoming new vessels for his glory.

Thankful for the Holy Spirit that teaches us and directs us to understand GOD'S Word for transformation, glory to GOD. A gift we are unworthy enough to receive but because of favor, because of his Love we are redeemed hallelujah!

Journaling

_____

_____

_____

_____

_____

_____

_____

_____

_____

_____

_____

_____

_____

_____

Psalm 55:22, NIV:

Cast your cares on the LORD and he will sustain you;
he will never let the righteous be shaken.

The GOD who controls all things will be there to protect and guide us in our fears or in any situation we may face. Our worries, fear, shame, doubt, none of it is too much for our GOD to bear. He is our El Elyon, hallelujah GOD!

Furthermore, when we cast everything that concerns us on him, He will sustain you! This means in our fear and anxiety, he will give us calmness, he will give us peace, regardless of what is going on around us.

GOD wants us to know and be in confidence that we can always depend on him. He is our rock, our fortress our deliverer whom we can take refuge. He is our shield and the horn of our salvation, our stronghold.

Our father is faithful and will sustain us giving us power and strength! Lean on him.

Journaling

_____

_____

_____

_____

_____

_____

_____

_____

_____

_____

_____

_____

_____

_____

Luke 2:7, NIV:

and she gave birth to her firstborn, a son. She wrapped him in cloths and placed him in a manger, because there was no guest room available for them.

Hebrews 13:8, NIV:

Jesus Christ is the same yesterday and today and forever.

Isaiah 40:28, NIV:

Do you not know? Have you not heard?
The Lord is the everlasting God, the Creator of the ends of the earth.
He will not grow tired or weary,
and his understanding no one can fathom.

Father even though there was no room for our savior to be in the comfort of the inn and he had to be in the manger, His birth being conducted in such conditions is yet another example of your agape Love especially noted to the least and the left out.

This is why I rejoice and am so glad that You reign My LORD. Thank you for your love and coming to relieve all oppression from JESUS birth till times of today. Thank you that, "Jesus Christ is the same yesterday and today and forever." we can always depend on him no matter the times Thank you Father for always stepping in to heal and give a future and a hope. Thank you for being our LORD the everlasting God, you are our Creator of the ends of the earth who will not grow tired or weary and has understanding that no one can fathom (). Always at the rescue restoring dignity and releasing peace.

Every day we are witness to the world being ruled by power, lust, and greed. but I am so glad today to be one in your Kingdom, which is ruled by Love, Compassion, and Mercy. Hallelujah God bless your Holy name!

Journaling

_____

_____

_____

_____

_____

_____

_____

_____

_____

_____

_____

_____

_____

_____

_____

John 11:25, NIV:

Jesus said to her, "I am the resurrection and the life. The one who believes in me will live, even though they die.

Believe in the resurrection of Christ JESUS, who was dead and buried but rose again on the third day. JESUS is alive and seated at the right hand of the father. Believe that once JESUS is accepted in our hearts, there is assurance that allows is to have confidence of the promise of eternal life which is beyond the grave. Believe that with JESUS, he is our life, our hope, and our eternal joy. Believe that being humble walking in obedience to his will, his word, grants acknowledgement in display of our love toward JESUS. Believe in JESUS through he may be dead, yet shall he live, believe.

Journaling

_____

_____

_____

_____

_____

_____

_____

_____

_____

_____

_____

_____

_____

_____

_____

_____

Encouragement

Our GOD is in the restoration business, and the Bible says that if we but confess our sins that he is faithful and just to forgive us of our sins and cleanse us of all unrighteousness. God will create in us a new heart and renew a right spirit within us, and I Decree and Declare that our Father is restoring you! I Decree and Declare that in this process of cleansing, of breaking down, he is chipping away, he is molding, he is shaping, and he is growing you! You were fearfully and wonderfully made! Sometimes we go down into the wilderness to the land of Egypt, and we get beat up and come out of there with the residue from the experience of being there. GOD had mercy and extended his grace, because he could have killed a lot of us when we were out in the wilderness. But he did not. He extended his hand of grace and now it is time for the cleanup, time to create in you what "He" needs of you for his plan that he has in store for you. To use you for his glory!

It does not matter what people think all that matters is what God thinks! If you are pleasing him, you be happy with you, you Be Good to You! Always remember JESUS Loves you! He is always there for you and you best believe you can always count on him to protect you. You can always lean on Him! Believe in him, he is our strong tower, our rock and our sustainer, and there's NOBODY LIKE OUR GOD! He is our strength that we can always run to in a time of trouble. You just must believe in him to do it as he has always done for you in the past. He will do it again! Trust Him, Pray to Him, He's waiting on you and I am Praying for you too! Now I pray that your sleep be sweet tonight. GOD Bless!

Psalm 57:2, ESV:

I cry out to God Most High,
to God who fulfills his purpose for me.

We all have a purpose and GOD has a plan.

Journaling

_____
_____
_____
_____
_____
_____
_____
_____
_____
_____
_____
_____
_____
_____
_____

Prayer

Thank you, LORD, for your divine touch, your strength, for breathing on us Father waking us up this morning, also when we become weak from the wears and tears of life father your there to rejuvenate us. Thank you for your protection, thank you for the blood, the blood of JESUS which makes us whole. Deposit into us your divine intellect. Help us to spiritually see you right there where you are at father so that we learn to come to you because go anywhere You never leave us father during the trying times of our lives, and we can be in confidence that our fears will be diminish, we can be in confidence as we walk with you that the enemy has lead way in our lives but that you direct our paths my LORD and you are our savior . Help us to Pray more to JESUS and put our hopes and trust with him.

Now to him who is able to do exceedingly and abundantly above all then we could ask or think, according to the power that works in us to him be glory in the church by CHRIST JESUS, to all generations forever and ever Amen, Amen, and Amen!

Romans 6:23, NIV:

For the wages of sin is death, but the gift of God is eternal life in[a]
Christ Jesus our Lord.

It is incomprehensible to me why anyone would not want to take advantage of having the gift of external life that is offered through our LORD and Savior JESUS CHRIST. He is our rock, our Jehovah Shalom (Peace), Our hope. Our advocate, Our Jehovah Nissi (Our banner), Our high priest, and Our Intercessor (just to name a few).

Being estranged from this gift and risk death is quite hard to apprehend. The true Holiness of this season should be the reason of celebration. The most precious gift of life is believing in JESUS and obtaining a relationship with him. The gift of salvation which is the best truth we could ever obtain in our lives that we all truly cannot "Live" without. I pray for blinded eyes to be open, ears to hear, and hearts to be softened this Christmas season.

I decree and declare that the pure joy of Christmas be a radiation through all the saints expelling the darkness in all that we may encounter daily.

Father GOD allow the pure joy of this holiday season to flow through us all in the body of CHRIST for Kingdom magnification and edification. In JESUS name I pray, Amen!

Journaling

_____
_____
_____
_____
_____
_____
_____
_____
_____
_____
_____
_____
_____
_____
_____

Printed in the United States
by Baker & Taylor Publisher Services